PLANET EARTH

MARK PETTIGREW

Stargazer Books

© Aladdin Books Ltd 2005

This edition published in the United States in 2005 by:
Stargazer Books
c/o The Creative Company
123 South Broad Street
P.O. Box 227
Mankato, Minnesota 56002

Editor: Katie Harker

Designer: Pete Bennett – PBD

Picture Researcher:
Brian Hunter Smart

Illustrator:
Louise Nevett

Printed in UAE

Library of Congress Cataloging-in-Publication Data

Pettigrew, Mark.
    Planet earth / by Mark Pettigrew.
       p. cm. -- (Science world)
    Includes index.
    ISBN 1-932799-28-1 (alk. paper)
    1. Earth--Juvenile literature.
    I. Title. II. Science world (North Mankato, Minn.)

QB631.4.P47 2004
551—dc22

                    2004041734

CONTENTS

*I*NTRODUCTION

Planet Earth is our home. It is also home to millions of different plants and animals. Like the human race, the planet Earth has a history—only many millions of years longer.

In this book you will discover how the earth began, what it is like today, and how it is changing. You will also see how movements in the earth's surface produce mountains, earthquakes, and volcanoes.

The Utah Desert—deserts cover a fifth of the earth's surface.

Have you ever wondered why the day is light and the night is dark? Or what causes leaves to fall from trees, the sun to rise, or the tides to change? Find out how the movement of our planet around the sun causes different patterns for life on Earth, and how the earth's climate has evolved throughout the planet's history.

The earth's oceans are home to many different species of wildlife.

PLANET EARTH

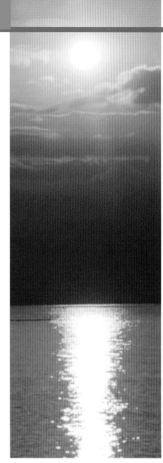

When you look out to sea, the horizon (or skyline) seems curved. This is because our planet is shaped like a ball; it measures about 8,000 miles across. The land and water that you see are only a small part of the earth's surface. Seen from space, Earth appears perfectly round with a smooth surface. The highest mountain is 29,000 ft high, and the deepest ocean is about 36,000 ft deep. These distances are very small compared to the size of the earth.

The earth is one of many planets in our solar system. But it is the only planet that has the right conditions for human life. Other planets are too cold or too hot for us to live there, or their atmospheres are too poisonous.

Planet Earth is made up of the atmosphere,

...the land,

...and the oceans.

THE EARTH'S ORIGIN

The earth was formed over 4.6 billion years ago. We believe that Earth and the other planets were formed from a flat gas cloud around the sun. This cloud formed into small, cold particles that attracted each other, collided, and formed larger particles. This took place over a few million years. As the larger particles collided, they became hot, and melted. Iron from these formed the central core of the earth, and other substances surrounded it.

The molten outer layer of the earth cooled to form a thin shell. Sometimes, molten rock escaped from under the surface in volcanic eruptions, as it still does today. Gases escaped from inside the earth to form an "atmosphere."

Structure of the earth

The outer layer of the earth is a thin, solid skin, called the "crust." Below it is a region called the "mantle." The outer layer of the mantle is made of molten rock, called "magma." Below the mantle is a region of molten rock under great pressure. The central region of the earth is a solid core.

Scientists predict that the temperature within the earth's core is about 10,800°F (6,000°C). They have studied temperature changes at different depths beneath the earth's surface and also believe that the melting point of iron—found near the earth's central core—is a good indication.

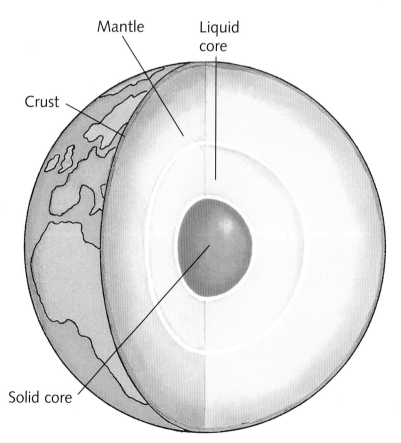

The most familiar type of volcano is a crater at the top of a steep summit.

Some volcanoes erupt regularly, while others are only active every hundred years or so.

CHANGING EARTH

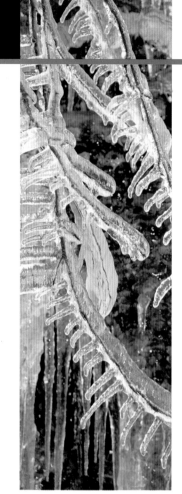

The remains of ancient animals, or "fossils," tell us that our planet and the life on it were once very different. Throughout the ages, the earth and its climate have changed, sometimes dramatically—as in the ice ages. The most recent ice age began 70,000 years ago, and lasted for 60,000 years.

Plants and animals living on Earth have adapted to the changes of our planet, to improve their chances of survival. Sometimes, plants and animals have also caused changes to the earth. For example, the soil in your backyard was partly formed from the rotting remains of dead plants and animals, called "humus."

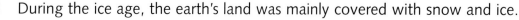

During the ice age, the earth's land was mainly covered with snow and ice.

The earth in a day

Imagine the changes of the earth's lifetime, squashed to fit into a 24-hour day. On this scale, there would be no life on Earth until about 6:30am, when the first microscopic plants and animals would appear. Large animals with backbones, like fish, would not appear until about 9:15pm. The first plants would appear at about 9:45pm, and some fish would take to the land at 10:00pm. Reptiles would appear at about 10:30pm. Dinosaurs and early mammals would be living on Earth at about 11pm, but mammals would only become common at 11:40pm. People would appear on Earth 40 seconds before midnight, and the first written history would be documented ten seconds before midnight.

MOVING CONTINENTS

The earth's crust is relatively thin, and is formed of large, flat pieces, called "plates." Each crustal plate may be thousands of miles across. These plates are moved very slowly by movements of the magma underneath. Where two plates push against each other, the crust crumples to form mountains. Where they move apart, magma can escape to form new rocks. Originally, the earth's land was close together, but over time the crustal plates have moved the land apart.

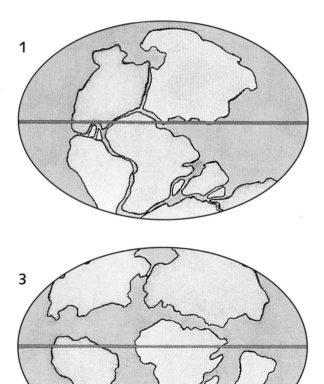

1

2

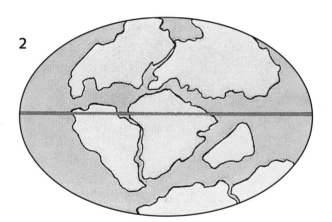

3

4

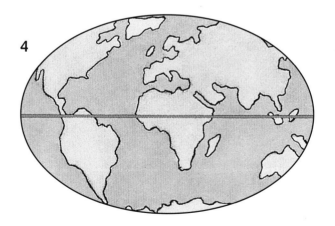

Changing times

200 million years ago the main land masses that we know today were all grouped close together (1). Over many millions of years, crustal plates carrying the continents have moved away from each other (2). 65 million years ago the continents had moved even farther apart (3). Today, the continents are still moving a few inches each year (4). The coastlines are also being slowly eroded by the sea. How will the continents look in 100 million years time?

When crustal plates press against each other, they do not slide smoothly. Instead, they push and push until suddenly they break at a weak point. As they break, there is a sudden movement of the crust, which we feel as an earthquake.

Occasionally, some of the mantle can push through weak points in the crust, and form a volcano. The crust is usually weaker along or near the lines where plates meet.

Earthquakes can cause a great deal of destruction.

Two crustal plates pushed against each other to form the Sierra Nevada Mountains.

ROCKS AND EROSION

Rocks are not as permanent as they seem. Rain, wind, and freezing weather can cause them to break up over a period of time. Tiny pieces of rock are washed away by rain and rivers. This process is called "erosion." Where rivers slow down or meet the sea, the rock fragments settle, forming a "sediment," such as sand or mud. Layers of sediment gradually thicken and the tiny pieces of rock become stuck together to form larger rocks. These are called "sedimentary" rocks.

Erosion and sedimentation are slow processes. They may take thousands of years to have a noticeable effect on the landscape around us.

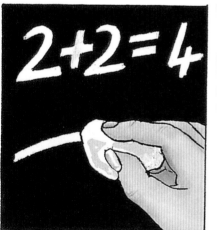

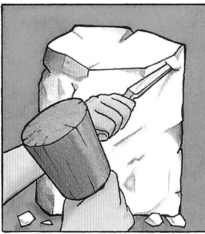

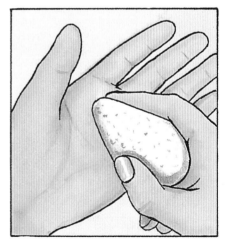

Sedimentary rocks

"Sedimentary" rocks are made of layers of small particles. For example, chalk cliffs are made from layers of very small shells and skeletons of sea animals.

Metamorphic rocks

Sedimentary rocks are changed when they are subjected to heat and pressure near a volcano. This is how "metamorphic" rocks, like marble, are formed.

Igneous rocks

"Igneous" rocks are formed from magma that has cooled, either slowly inside the earth, or quickly on the surface. Pumice and granite form like this.

Rock shapes like the Delicate Arch in Utah are formed by erosion.

RICHES OF THE EARTH

All the metals we use are taken from the earth. Most of them are found in rocks, combined with other substances. Others, such as gold and copper, are found as pure metal. Many of the "fossil fuels" we use, like coal, gas, and oil, are also taken from the earth. Coal is usually dug out of the ground, while gas and oil are extracted by drilling deep holes in the earth.

Rocks in the earth's crust are often used for specialized jobs. For example, one rock called "mica" is found in thin transparent sheets. It can be used to make windows for high-temperature ovens in which glass windows would melt.

How coal was formed

Coal was formed over millions of years from the remains of ancient forests growing on swamps (1). As forest trees and plants died, they fell into the swamps, forming layers of dead vegetation. Sedimentary rocks later formed on top of these layers (2).

Coal is a fossil fuel often mined from underground.

The pressure caused by the rocks made the layers of vegetation dense and hard (3), and formed them into a solid rock—coal (4).

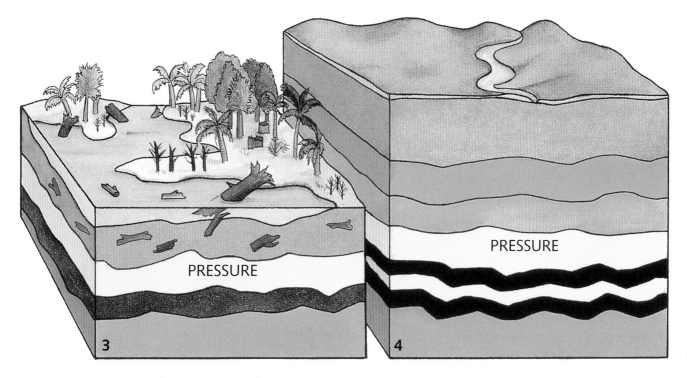

EARTH'S OCEANS

The oceans cover about two-thirds of the earth's surface and have existed for more than three billion years!

The top layer of the ocean has a rich plant and animal life, called "plankton." Millions of these tiny organisms are food for all the other sea animals. Plankton is one of the oldest forms of life on Earth. Deeper down, at about three hundred feet, it is too dark for plants to grow, so the ocean bottom is mostly bare.

Winds blowing across the ocean cause waves. When winds blow over a great distance across the sea, they build waves that may be many feet tall.

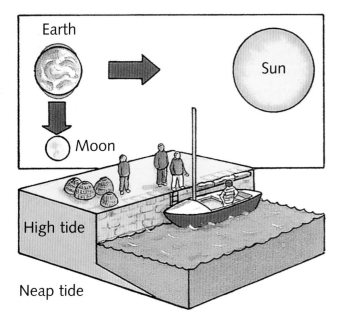
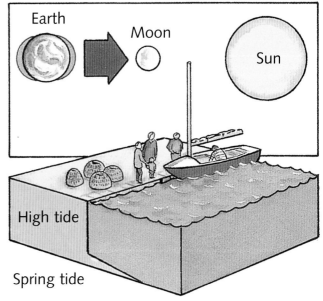

The tides

Tides are caused by the pull of the moon and the sun on the waters of the earth. When both the sun and moon are in line with the earth, their pulls combine and the tides are very large. These are called "spring tides." When the sun and moon are out of line with the earth, their pulls oppose each other, and the tides are not as large. These are called "neap tides."

Cannon Beach, Oregon—the action of the waves can cause erosion of the coastline.

The Papua New Guinea islands surrounded by the Pacific Ocean—Earth's largest ocean.

SPINNING EARTH

The sun appears to us as if it moves around the earth. In fact, the earth spins around on its axis like a top, once every day. The place where you live faces the sun during the day, and away from it at night.

The earth spins on its axis at a great speed: the surface of the earth moves at more than 900mph. Gravity provides the force that prevents us from falling off the earth. Gravity extends a long way from the earth, and pulls anything within its range toward the earth. The moon and artificial satellites are held in orbit around the earth by the pull of its gravity.

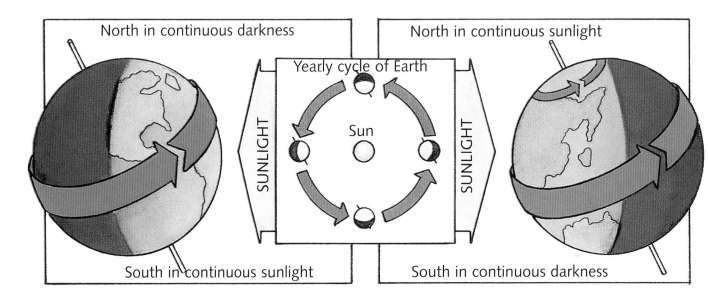

The seasons

The seasons are caused by the earth's orbit around the sun. The diagram shows how the earth's axis is slanted. During summer in the northern world, the midday sun is over a region north of the equator, so its rays are more concentrated and feel hotter. During winter, the sun is over a region south of the equator, and the rays reaching the north cover a larger area. They are less concentrated, so they feel less hot. Places south of the equator have their summer when places north of the equator have winter.

As the earth spins, different seasons occur in different parts of the world. Daylight hours increase in the summer and decrease in the winter, weather patterns differ, animals alter their behavior as the temperature changes, and plants adapt to suit their new surroundings. The four seasons— spring, summer, fall, and winter— occur at similar times each year.

The warm, sunny climate of summer

The cold and wet climate of winter

CLIMATE

Different parts of the globe have very different climates. It gets hotter as you travel toward the equator because the sun's rays are more concentrated there. Places near the sea are usually cooler in the summer, and warmer in winter, than places inland. This is because the sea heats up and cools down less easily than the land, so it keeps the land near the sea warm in winter and cool in summer.

These differences in temperature cause movements of air across the earth's surface, called winds. Air movements, in turn, cause clouds and rain to form, as warm, moist air is cooled as it rises up over hills.

Arctic Circle

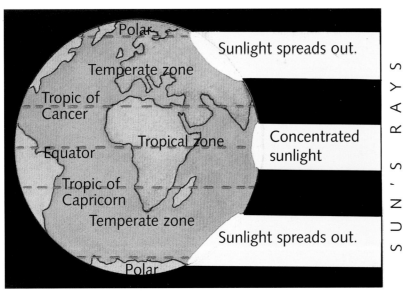

Antarctic Circle

The sun's rays travel about 90 million miles (150 million km) to reach the earth, providing our planet with light and heat. By rotating once every 24 hours, the earth keeps the distribution of heat and light balanced with regular alternating periods of daylight and darkness.

The diagram above shows how the sun's rays fall at both the equator and the poles. At the equator, the sun's rays are spread over a smaller area than rays reaching the earth at the poles. This means that sunlight reaching polar regions is less intense than sunlight reaching the equator. It also means that places near the poles are cooler than places near the equator.

The two poles are covered in snow and ice and temperatures drop dramatically.

The hottest and driest climates on Earth are found in the deserts.

THE ATMOSPHERE

The air you breathe forms a thin layer around the earth, known as the "atmosphere." This stretches up for a few hundred miles. As you go higher, there is less air. At the height at which planes fly, there is too little air to breathe.

Most plants and animals need atmospheric gases in order to survive. Animals rely on oxygen to breathe, and plants rely on carbon dioxide to make their food. The air also contains nitrogen, small amounts of other gases, and some water vapor and dust. The "stratosphere" and "ionosphere" contain small amounts of "ozone," which is a form of oxygen. A layer of ozone prevents harmful ultraviolet rays from the sun reaching the earth's surface.

The aurora are caused by charged particles from the sun hitting the atmosphere.

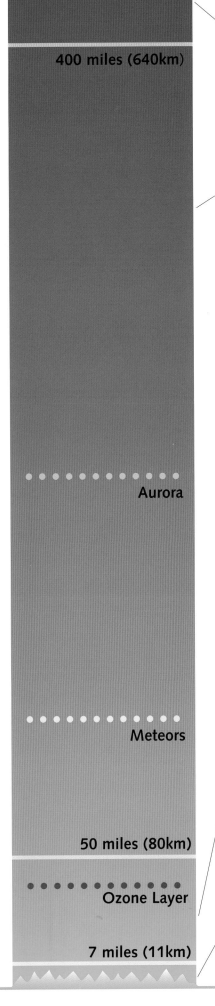

400 miles (640km)

Aurora

Meteors

50 miles (80km)

Ozone Layer

7 miles (11km)

Exosphere

The highest, outer region of the earth's atmosphere is called the "exosphere." Here, conditions are not very different from outer space as there is very little air.

Ionosphere

The "ionosphere" is made up of electrically charged particles, produced when radiation from the sun hits the upper atmosphere. Near the poles, this causes a brilliant display of lights, the "aurora borealis" (northern lights) and the "aurora australis" (southern lights).

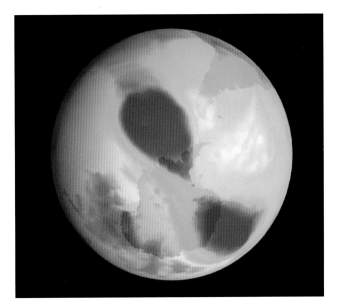

Manmade pollution has caused a hole to appear in the ozone layer (above).

Stratosphere

The "stratosphere" extends up to about 50 miles (80km) above Earth. As you travel upward in this layer, the temperature rises slightly. Nevertheless, temperatures are below freezing point.

Troposphere

The "troposphere" contains the air we breathe. Clouds, rain, and snow all form in this layer. As you travel up through the troposphere, it becomes colder.

EARTH'S BALANCE

The parts of the world that affect our lives are called the "environment." This includes the earth's crust and land, oceans, atmosphere, plants, and animals. If the balance between things added and things taken away from the environment is upset, the environment will change.

Many of the things we take from the earth, like metals and fossil fuels, take millions of years to be replaced naturally. Other things, such as wood from trees, are replaced more quickly, but if we use them too fast, they will disappear. Some things we produce, like poisons and waste, are not removed as quickly as we add them to the environment, so they build up as pollution.

 The U.S. produces 230 million tons of household waste each year.

Cutting down huge forests can cause changes in the earth's atmosphere.

Pollution from industry can also disturb the earth's balance.

MAKE YOUR OWN ORRERY

An "orrery" is a model that shows how the planets move in their orbits around the sun. In this model you can see how the earth travels around the sun and how, at the same time, the moon travels around the earth. The planets are not made to any realistic scale as the sun is many thousands of times larger than the earth.

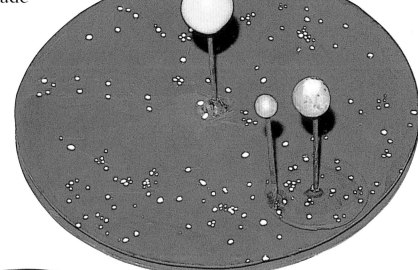

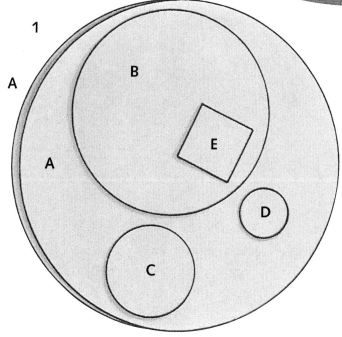

What you need
3 toothpicks
Thin white cardboard
Thumbtack
Modeling clay
Scissors
Compass
Ruler

1. Draw five circles using a compass, and a square, to the measurements listed below. Cut out the shapes from the cardboard.

A=3.7in (95mm)   B=2.4in (60mm)   C=0.9in (23mm)   D=0.5in (12mm)   E=1.6x1.6in
radius (x 2)   radius   radius   radius   (40x40mm)

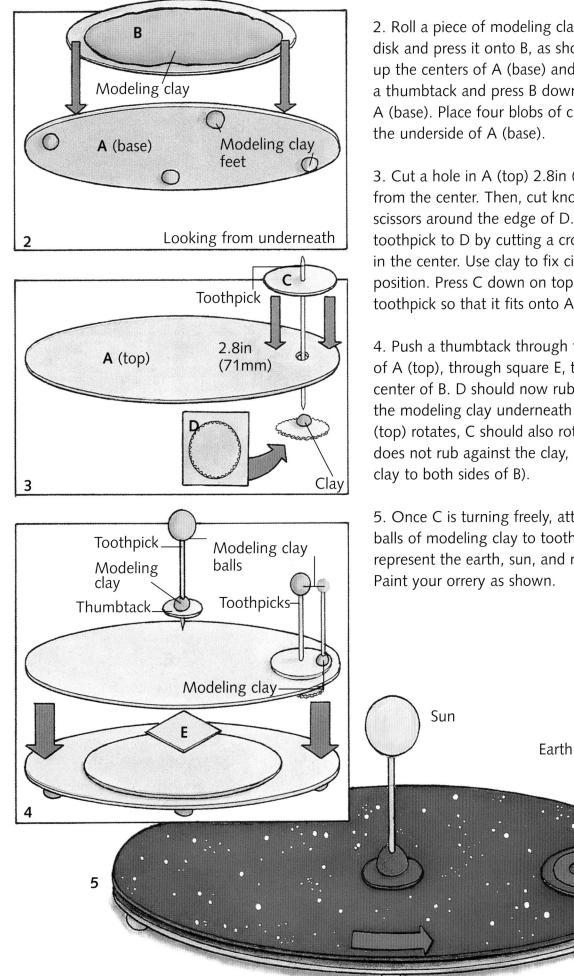

2 — Looking from underneath

B
Modeling clay

A (base)
Modeling clay feet

3

Toothpick
C
A (top)
2.8in (71mm)
D
Clay

4

Toothpick
Modeling clay balls
Modeling clay
Thumbtack
Toothpicks
Modeling clay
E

5

Sun
Earth   Moon

2. Roll a piece of modeling clay into a flat disk and press it onto B, as shown. Line up the centers of A (base) and B with a thumbtack and press B down onto A (base). Place four blobs of clay on the underside of A (base).

3. Cut a hole in A (top) 2.8in (71mm) from the center. Then, cut knotches using scissors around the edge of D. Attach a toothpick to D by cutting a cross shape in the center. Use clay to fix circle D in position. Press C down on top of a toothpick so that it fits onto A (top).

4. Push a thumbtack through the center of A (top), through square E, to the center of B. D should now rub against the modeling clay underneath B. As A (top) rotates, C should also rotate. (If D does not rub against the clay, add more clay to both sides of B).

5. Once C is turning freely, attach small balls of modeling clay to toothpicks to represent the earth, sun, and moon. Paint your orrery as shown.

MORE ABOUT PLANET EARTH

Moving crust

As the plates of the earth's surface move toward each other, one plate may rise over another. The one that moves up forms mountains, and the one that moves down is slowly melted below the earth's surface. Where two plates move away from each other, magma is free to escape. It solidifies to form rock, and a "mid-ocean ridge" or a "volcanic island" is formed.

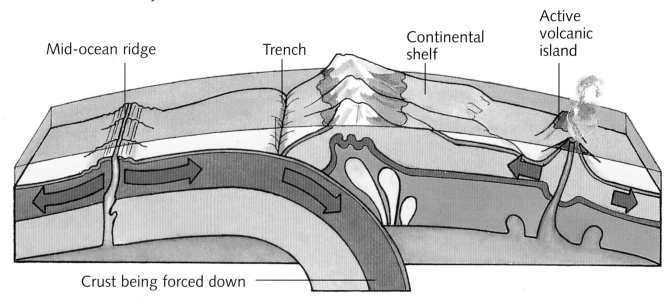

Mid-ocean ridge

Trench

Continental shelf

Active volcanic island

Crust being forced down

Folding

Movements in the earth's plates can also cause the earth's surface to buckle and split. Where the surface splits and slips, a "fault" is produced. Where the surface buckles, a "fold" is formed. Many familiar features of the landscape are caused by folds and faults, and these can often be seen in layers of rocks at seaside cliffs. The diagram shows some of the features that can be produced in these ways.

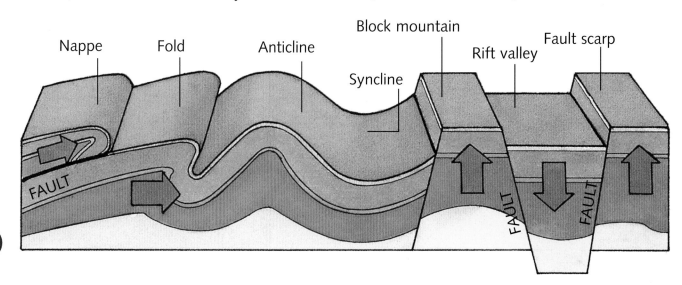

Nappe

Fold

Anticline

Syncline

Block mountain

Rift valley

Fault scarp

FAULT

FAULT

FAULT

GLOSSARY

Atmosphere
The layers of air surrounding the earth.

Aurora
A display of lights seen in the sky near the north and south poles, caused by charged particles from the sun hitting the atmosphere.

Axis
An imaginary line from the north pole to the south pole around which the earth spins.

Climate
The usual weather conditions of a region of the earth throughout the year.

Continental drift
The slow movement of the continental plates over millions of years.

Core
The center of the earth, made up of solid metallic rock surrounded by molten rock.

Crust
The solid surface skin of the earth. It floats on a layer of fluid rock called the mantle.

Crustal plates
Large flat plates, thousands of miles across, that make up the surface of the earth.

Environment
The parts of the earth where we live. The environment includes the crust, land, atmosphere, oceans, plants, and animals.

Erosion
The gradual wearing away of weathered rocks by the action of wind, rain, rivers, and the sea.

Fossils
The remains of ancient animals that have been buried under layers of sand or mud for millions of years.

Gravity
Everything on the earth, or nearby, is pulled toward the center of the earth. This pull is called gravity.

Ice Age
A period of time when much of the earth's surface was covered for thousands of years by a thick layer of ice. During the last ice age, much of North America was covered by ice.

Igneous rocks
Rocks that are formed from magma which has cooled, either slowly inside the earth, or quickly on the surface of the earth.

Magma
Molten rock found beneath the surface of the earth.

Mantle
The region of the earth's interior beneath the crust. Just below the crust, the mantle is molten, but it becomes more solid several hundred miles down.

Metamorphic rocks
Sedimentary rocks that have been subjected to heat and pressure, causing a change in their chemical structure.

Plankton
Microscopic plants and animals that live in the top few yards of the oceans. They provide food for many sea animals.

Pollution
Things like poisons and garbage that humans add to the environment faster than they can be removed.

Sediment
Small particles that settle as a layer when fast-moving water carrying sand or mud slows down.

Sedimentary rocks
Rocks made of layers of small particles.

INDEX

Photocredits Abbreviations: l-left, r-right, b-bottom, t-top, c-center, m-middle. Front cover main, front cover mt, 7b, 8tr, 9 both, 12tr, 20tr, 24tr, 26tr, 27t — Digital Stock. front cover mb, 2tl, 3tr, 4tl, 5tr, 6 all, 8tl, 10tl, 10b, 12 both 14tl, 16 both, 18 both, 20tl, 22tl, 23 both, 24tl, 24b, 26tl, 28tl, 30t, 31t, 32t — Corbis. 1, 2-3, 4-5, 7t, 13b, 19t, 22tr — Photodisc. 4tr, 19b — Photoessentials. 13tr — FEMA. 14tr — Corel. 15 — Zefa. 17t — Roger Ressmeyer/CORBIS. 21t — Tony Stone. 21bl, 21br — K. Harker. 25r — NASA. 26b — B. H. Smart. 27b — Rex Features. 28tr — NSSDC & NASA.